Carrots for April the Bunny

Buffalo Dance

Modal Study

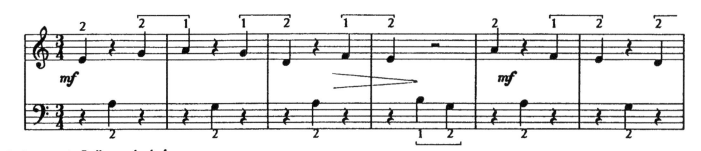

Bring out R.H. melody!

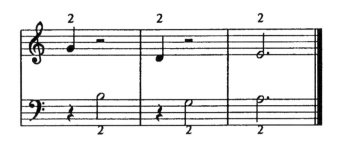

Bells Ringing

Waltz for Mo & May

Carillon

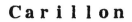

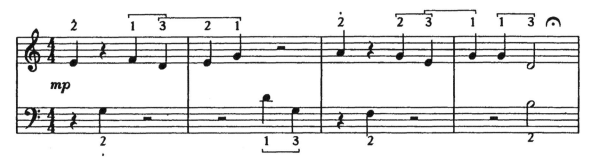

Somersaults

Chorale

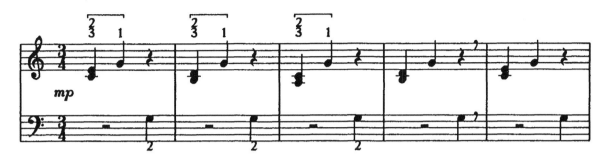

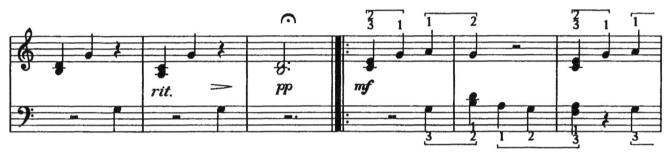

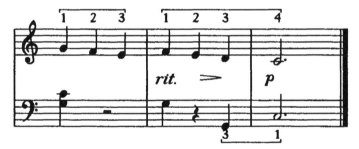

Azaleas in Houston

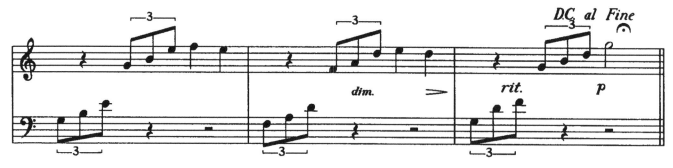

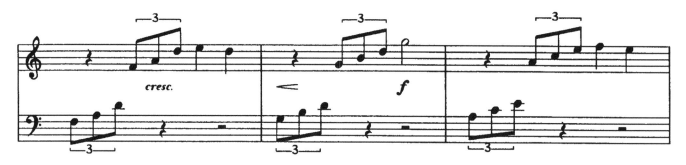

Japanese Lanterns

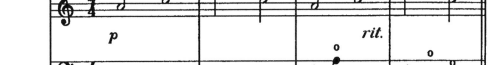

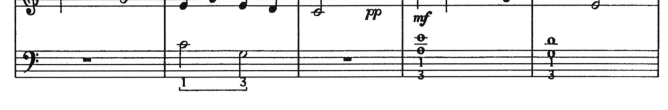

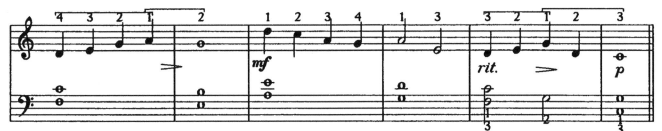

Goldfish

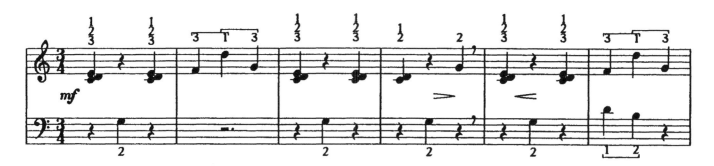

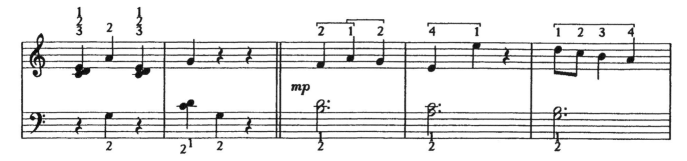

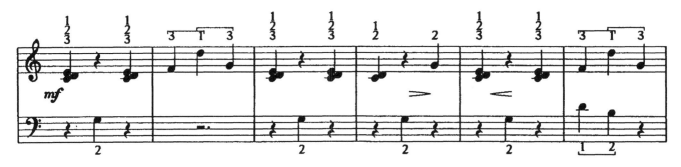

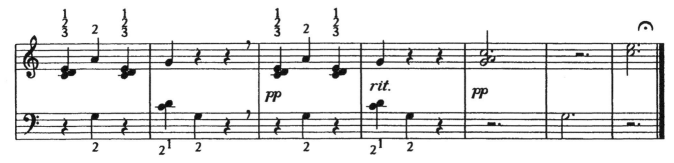

Roller-Skating with Friends

Waterlilies

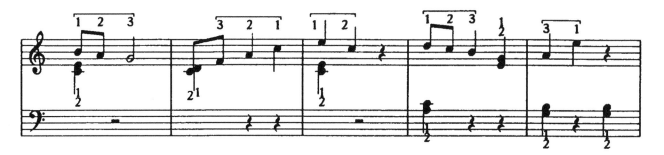

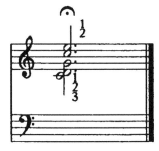

Motor Cat

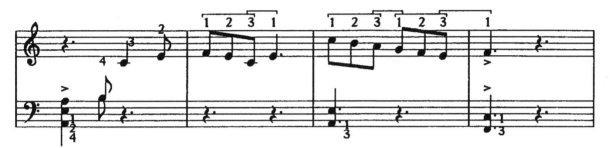

© 1993 Bel Artes Press

Bee Keeping

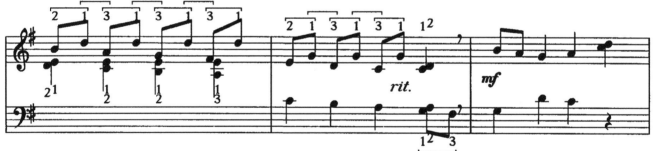

Bridge with Chinese Dragons

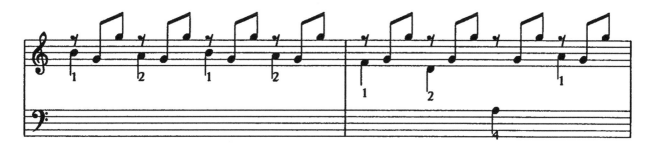